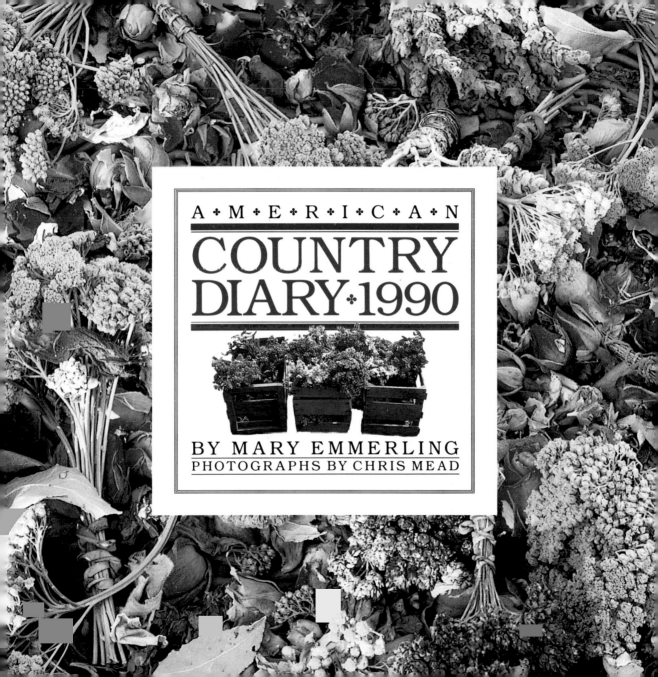

A · M · E · R · I · C · A · N

COUNTRY DIARY · 1990

BY MARY EMMERLING
PHOTOGRAPHS BY CHRIS MEAD

Workman Publishing Company
708 Broadway
New York, New York 10003

Printed in Japan
First printing August 1989

ISBN: 0-89480-739-0

It has been ten years since my book *American Country* was published and six years since the first American Country Diary came out. Everyone said that country wouldn't last, that it was a fad. I am glad to say that country is stronger than ever and it has been a wonderful ten years. With the way I see people collecting antiques, decorating their homes all in country, and using the *American Country* books and Diary for ideas, I would say country is forever!

Happy Country Days to each and every one of you.

MARY EMMERLING

1990

JANUARY
S	M	T	W	T	F	S
	1	2	3	4	5	6
7	8	9	10	11	12	13
14	15	16	17	18	19	20
21	22	23	24	25	26	27
28	29	30	31			

FEBRUARY
S	M	T	W	T	F	S
				1	2	3
4	5	6	7	8	9	10
11	12	13	14	15	16	17
18	19	20	21	22	23	24
25	26	27	28			

MARCH
S	M	T	W	T	F	S
				1	2	3
4	5	6	7	8	9	10
11	12	13	14	15	16	17
18	19	20	21	22	23	24
25	26	27	28	29	30	31

APRIL
S	M	T	W	T	F	S
1	2	3	4	5	6	7
8	9	10	11	12	13	14
15	16	17	18	19	20	21
22	23	24	25	26	27	28
29	30					

MAY
S	M	T	W	T	F	S
		1	2	3	4	5
6	7	8	9	10	11	12
13	14	15	16	17	18	19
20	21	22	23	24	25	26
27	28	29	30	31		

JUNE
S	M	T	W	T	F	S
					1	2
3	4	5	6	7	8	9
10	11	12	13	14	15	16
17	18	19	20	21	22	23
24	25	26	27	28	29	30

JULY
S	M	T	W	T	F	S
1	2	3	4	5	6	7
8	9	10	11	12	13	14
15	16	17	18	19	20	21
22	23	24	25	26	27	28
29	30	31				

AUGUST
S	M	T	W	T	F	S
			1	2	3	4
5	6	7	8	9	10	11
12	13	14	15	16	17	18
19	20	21	22	23	24	25
26	27	28	29	30	31	

SEPTEMBER
S	M	T	W	T	F	S
						1
2	3	4	5	6	7	8
9	10	11	12	13	14	15
16	17	18	19	20	21	22
23/30	24	25	26	27	28	29

OCTOBER
S	M	T	W	T	F	S
	1	2	3	4	5	6
7	8	9	10	11	12	13
14	15	16	17	18	19	20
21	22	23	24	25	26	27
28	29	30	31			

NOVEMBER
S	M	T	W	T	F	S
				1	2	3
4	5	6	7	8	9	10
11	12	13	14	15	16	17
18	19	20	21	22	23	24
25	26	27	28	29	30	

DECEMBER
S	M	T	W	T	F	S
						1
2	3	4	5	6	7	8
9	10	11	12	13	14	15
16	17	18	19	20	21	22
23/30	24/31	25	26	27	28	29

1991

JANUARY

S	M	T	W	T	F	S
		1	2	3	4	5
6	7	8	9	10	11	12
13	14	15	16	17	18	19
20	21	22	23	24	25	26
27	28	29	30	31		

FEBRUARY

S	M	T	W	T	F	S
					1	2
3	4	5	6	7	8	9
10	11	12	13	14	15	16
17	18	19	20	21	22	23
24	25	26	27	28		

MARCH

S	M	T	W	T	F	S
					1	2
3	4	5	6	7	8	9
10	11	12	13	14	15	16
17	18	19	20	21	22	23
24/31	25	26	27	28	29	30

APRIL

S	M	T	W	T	F	S
	1	2	3	4	5	6
7	8	9	10	11	12	13
14	15	16	17	18	19	20
21	22	23	24	25	26	27
28	29	30				

MAY

S	M	T	W	T	F	S
			1	2	3	4
5	6	7	8	9	10	11
12	13	14	15	16	17	18
19	20	21	22	23	24	25
26	27	28	29	30	31	

JUNE

S	M	T	W	T	F	S
						1
2	3	4	5	6	7	8
9	10	11	12	13	14	15
16	17	18	19	20	21	22
23/30	24	25	26	27	28	29

JULY

S	M	T	W	T	F	S
	1	2	3	4	5	6
7	8	9	10	11	12	13
14	15	16	17	18	19	20
21	22	23	24	25	26	27
28	29	30	31			

AUGUST

S	M	T	W	T	F	S
				1	2	3
4	5	6	7	8	9	10
11	12	13	14	15	16	17
18	19	20	21	22	23	24
25	26	27	28	29	30	31

SEPTEMBER

S	M	T	W	T	F	S
1	2	3	4	5	6	7
8	9	10	11	12	13	14
15	16	17	18	19	20	21
22	23	24	25	26	27	28
29	30					

OCTOBER

S	M	T	W	T	F	S
		1	2	3	4	5
6	7	8	9	10	11	12
13	14	15	16	17	18	19
20	21	22	23	24	25	26
27	28	29	30	31		

NOVEMBER

S	M	T	W	T	F	S
					1	2
3	4	5	6	7	8	9
10	11	12	13	14	15	16
17	18	19	20	21	22	23
24	25	26	27	28	29	30

DECEMBER

S	M	T	W	T	F	S
1	2	3	4	5	6	7
8	9	10	11	12	13	14
15	16	17	18	19	20	21
22	23	24	25	26	27	28
29	30	31				

Late nineteenth- and early twentieth-century advertising tins.

JANUARY

MONDAY
1
NEW YEAR'S DAY

FRIDAY
5

TUESDAY
2

SATURDAY
6

WEDNESDAY
3

SUNDAY
7

JANUARY

MONDAY
8

TUESDAY
9

WEDNESDAY
10

New England baskets and dried

flowers hanging on a pine cupboard.

<u>THURSDAY</u>
11

<u>FRIDAY</u>
12

<u>SATURDAY</u>
13

<u>SUNDAY</u>
14

JANUARY

THURSDAY
18

MONDAY
15
MARTIN LUTHER KING JR.'S BIRTHDAY

FRIDAY
19

TUESDAY
16

SATURDAY
20

WEDNESDAY
17

SUNDAY
21

Black-glazed redware from New England in a step-back cupboard.

JANUARY

<u>MONDAY</u>	
22	

<u>TUESDAY</u>	
23	

<u>WEDNESDAY</u>	
24	

A brightly colored baby quilt

and New England pantry box.

THURSDAY
25

FRIDAY
26

SATURDAY
27

SUNDAY
28

Wildflowers in an Ohio farmhouse.

JANUARY
FEBRUARY

MONDAY
29

TUESDAY
30

WEDNESDAY
31

THURSDAY
1

FRIDAY
2

SATURDAY
3

SUNDAY
4

FEBRUARY

THURSDAY
8

MONDAY
5

FRIDAY
9

TUESDAY
6

SATURDAY
10

WEDNESDAY
7

SUNDAY
11

Turn-of-the-century quilts draped over a balcony railing.

Hand-painted china from the

FEBRUARY

late 1800s in a kitchen cupboard.

THURSDAY	SATURDAY
15	**17**
FRIDAY	**SUNDAY**
16	**18**

FEBRUARY

MONDAY
19
PRESIDENTS DAY

TUESDAY
20

WEDNESDAY
21

Herbal wreaths on a

Connecticut barn door.

THURSDAY
22
WASHINGTON'S BIRTHDAY

FRIDAY
23

SATURDAY
24

SUNDAY
25

FEBRUARY
MARCH

MONDAY
26

TUESDAY
27

WEDNESDAY
28
ASH WEDNESDAY

Wallpaper-covered

hatboxes.

THURSDAY
1

FRIDAY
2

SATURDAY
3

SUNDAY
4

Pillows made from quilt pieces in a New York State wooden carrier.

MARCH

THURSDAY
8

MONDAY
5

TUESDAY
6

WEDNESDAY
7

FRIDAY
9

SATURDAY
10

SUNDAY
11

MARCH

THURSDAY
15

MONDAY
12

FRIDAY
16

TUESDAY
13

SATURDAY
17
ST. PATRICK'S DAY

WEDNESDAY
14

SUNDAY
18

Iron kitchen utensils in a Massachusetts saltbox kitchen.

MARCH

MONDAY
19

TUESDAY
20

WEDNESDAY
21

Texas antiques from the mid-

...nineteenth century, used for dining.

Shaker pantry boxes on a hanging shelf.

MARCH
APRIL

MONDAY
26

TUESDAY
27

WEDNESDAY
28

THURSDAY
29

FRIDAY
30

SATURDAY
31

SUNDAY
1

A Massachusetts chimney cupboard.

Daffodils in full bloom on an early spring morning.

APRIL

MONDAY
2

TUESDAY
3

WEDNESDAY
4

THURSDAY
5

FRIDAY
6

SATURDAY
7

SUNDAY
8
PALM SUNDAY

APRIL

<u>MONDAY</u>

9

<u>TUESDAY</u>

10

PASSOVER BEGINS

<u>WEDNESDAY</u>

11

Hand-carved wooden decoys

silhouetted in a window.

THURSDAY
12

FRIDAY
13
GOOD FRIDAY

SATURDAY
14

SUNDAY
15
EASTER

APRIL

MONDAY
16

TUESDAY
17

WEDNESDAY
18

THURSDAY
19

FRIDAY
20

SATURDAY
21

SUNDAY
22

A collection of dolls and children's wicker chairs.

Miniature carvings and old kitchen

APRIL

<u>MONDAY</u>
23

<u>TUESDAY</u>
24

<u>WEDNESDAY</u>
25

...utensils displayed on a shelf.

THURSDAY 26	SATURDAY 28
FRIDAY 27	SUNDAY 29

A forsythia hedge along a country fence.

APRIL
MAY

MONDAY
30

TUESDAY
1

WEDNESDAY
2

THURSDAY
3

FRIDAY
4

SATURDAY
5

SUNDAY
6

MAY

MONDAY
7

TUESDAY
8

WEDNESDAY
9

Tiger maple bed

c. 1820, from Ohio.

THURSDAY
10

F R I D A Y
11

SATURDAY
12

S U N D A Y
13
MOTHER'S DAY

A tin cooking collection

MAY

TUESDAY
15

MONDAY
14

WEDNESDAY
16

on a kitchen shelf.

THURSDAY 17	SATURDAY 19
FRIDAY 18	SUNDAY 20

MAY

THURSDAY
24

MONDAY
21

FRIDAY
25

TUESDAY
22

SATURDAY
26

WEDNESDAY
23

SUNDAY
27

Roses climbing a country picket fence on Long Island.

MAY
JUNE

<u>M O N D A Y</u>

28
MEMORIAL DAY OBSERVED

<u>T U E S D A Y</u>

29

<u>W E D N E S D A Y</u>

30
TRADITIONAL MEMORIAL DAY

A wagon wheel marking the

entrance to an old adobe home.

THURSDAY
31

FRIDAY
1

SATURDAY
2

SUNDAY
3

Wild country flowers in ironstone pitchers.

JUNE

THURSDAY
7

MONDAY
4

FRIDAY
8

TUESDAY
5

SATURDAY
9

WEDNESDAY
6

SUNDAY
10

JUNE

<u>MONDAY</u>

11

<u>TUESDAY</u>

12

<u>WEDNESDAY</u>

13

Mochaware mugs on a

Connecticut cupboard.

THURSDAY
14

FRIDAY
15

SATURDAY
16

SUNDAY
17
FATHER'S DAY

JUNE

THURSDAY
21

MONDAY
18

FRIDAY
22

TUESDAY
19

SATURDAY
23

WEDNESDAY
20

SUNDAY
24

Basket full of Midwestern quilts from the 1890s to 1930s.

JUNE
JULY

MONDAY
25

TUESDAY
26

WEDNESDAY
27

Maine birdhouse

in a country inn.

FRIDAY
29

SATURDAY
30

SUNDAY
1

A nineteenth-century cast iron and

JULY

MONDAY
2

TUESDAY
3

WEDNESDAY
4
INDEPENDENCE DAY

tin horse and carriage collection.

THURSDAY
5

SATURDAY
7

FRIDAY
6

SUNDAY
8

Vegetables at a roadside farm stand in Virginia.

JULY

MONDAY
9

TUESDAY
10

WEDNESDAY
11

THURSDAY
12

FRIDAY
13

SATURDAY
14

SUNDAY
15

William Meyer pottery from Texas in all shapes and sizes.

JULY

TUESDAY

17

MONDAY

16

WEDNESDAY

18

Farm baskets and hand-dipped candles.

THURSDAY 19	SATURDAY 21
FRIDAY 20	SUNDAY 22

JULY

MONDAY
23

TUESDAY
24

WEDNESDAY
25

A crib quilt with starburst

design in a Long Island barn.

FRIDAY
27

SATURDAY
28

SUNDAY
29

JULY
AUGUST

MONDAY
30

FRIDAY
3

TUESDAY
31

SATURDAY
4

WEDNESDAY
1

SUNDAY
5

An outdoor antique show in New England.

A garden room with blossoms and baskets.

AUGUST

THURSDAY
9

MONDAY
6

FRIDAY
10

TUESDAY
7

SATURDAY
11

WEDNESDAY
8

SUNDAY
12

AUGUST

MONDAY
13

TUESDAY
14

WEDNESDAY
15

New England store trade signs and barber

...oles from the 1800s and early 1900s.

THURSDAY
16

FRIDAY
17

SATURDAY
18

SUNDAY
19

AUGUST

MONDAY
20

TUESDAY
21

WEDNESDAY
22

THURSDAY
23

FRIDAY
24

SATURDAY
25

SUNDAY
26

A pie safe from the 1830s in a Texas farmhouse.

An Anglo-Texan pie safe from the 1830s.

AUGUST
SEPTEMBER

MONDAY
27

TUESDAY
28

WEDNESDAY
29

THURSDAY
30

FRIDAY
31

SATURDAY
1

SUNDAY
2

A collection of antique dishes in a Maine inn.

Harvested vegetables in country baskets.

SEPTEMBER

THURSDAY
6

MONDAY
3
LABOR DAY

FRIDAY
7

TUESDAY
4

SATURDAY
8

WEDNESDAY
5

SUNDAY
9
GRANDPARENTS DAY

SEPTEMBER

MONDAY 10
TUESDAY 11
<u>WEDNESDAY</u> 12

Indiana hickory chairs a

a Louisiana pine table.

THURSDAY
13

FRIDAY
14

SATURDAY
15

SUNDAY
16

Handcrafted stoneware from the late nineteenth century.

SEPTEMBER

MONDAY
17

TUESDAY
18

WEDNESDAY
19

A collection of storage and pickling jars.

<u>**THURSDAY**</u> **20** *ROSH HASHANAH*	<u>**SATURDAY**</u> **22**
<u>**FRIDAY**</u> **21**	<u>**SUNDAY**</u> **23**

SEPTEMBER

MONDAY
24

FRIDAY
28

TUESDAY
25

SATURDAY
29
YOM KIPPUR

WEDNESDAY
26

SUNDAY
30

A Long Island barn decorated with New England antiques and quilts.

The Mission House in Massachusetts, with its surrounding herb garden.

OCTOBER

MONDAY
1

TUESDAY
2

WEDNESDAY
3

THURSDAY
4

FRIDAY
5

SATURDAY
6

SUNDAY
7

OCTOBER

MONDAY
8
COLUMBUS DAY OBSERVED

TUESDAY
9

WEDNESDAY
10

Pine bed, c. 1870, with a quilt from the

nineteenth century, at Round Top, Texas.

THURSDAY
11

FRIDAY
12
TRADITIONAL COLUMBUS DAY

SATURDAY
13

SUNDAY
14

OCTOBER

THURSDAY
18

MONDAY
15

FRIDAY
19

TUESDAY
16

SATURDAY
20

WEDNESDAY
17

SUNDAY
21

A blue ladderback chair next to a painted nineteenth-century cupboard.

Texas pottery on

OCTOBER

a kitchen shelf.

THURSDAY 25	SATURDAY 27
FRIDAY 26	SUNDAY 28

OCTOBER
NOVEMBER

MONDAY
29

TUESDAY
30

WEDNESDAY
31
HALLOWEEN

Pumpkins and corn stalks

or a country Halloween.

THURSDAY
1

FRIDAY
2

SATURDAY
3

SUNDAY
4

NOVEMBER

MONDAY
5

TUESDAY
6
ELECTION DAY

WEDNESDAY
7

Kitchen copper molds

in a country cupboard.

NOVEMBER

THURSDAY
15

MONDAY
12

FRIDAY
16

TUESDAY
13

SATURDAY
17

WEDNESDAY
14

SUNDAY
18

Dried flowers in a Maine farmhouse.

Ornamental iron door stops, c. 1810.

NOVEMBER

MONDAY
19

TUESDAY
20

WEDNESDAY
21

Black memorabilia from the late nineteenth century.

THURSDAY **22** *THANKSGIVING*	**SATURDAY** **24**
F R I D A Y **23**	**S U N D A Y** **25**

Yellowware and Ohio blue bowls.

NOVEMBER
DECEMBER

MONDAY
26

TUESDAY
27

WEDNESDAY
28

THURSDAY
29

FRIDAY
30

SATURDAY
1

SUNDAY
2

Antique kitchenware in a pantry.

DECEMBER

MONDAY
3
TUESDAY
4
WEDNESDAY
5

Antique lace children's clothes

and an Ohio trundle bed.

THURSDAY
6

FRIDAY
7

SATURDAY
8

SUNDAY
9

DECEMBER

THURSDAY
13

MONDAY
10

FRIDAY
14

TUESDAY
11

SATURDAY
15

WEDNESDAY
12
HANUKKAH BEGINS

SUNDAY
16

New England pewter plates and hogscraper candlesticks.

DECEMBER

MONDAY
17

TUESDAY
18

WEDNESDAY
19

A well-loved hand-me-down

teddy bear with button eyes.

THURSDAY
20

FRIDAY
21

SATURDAY
22

SUNDAY
23

Christmas dinner at the Red Fox Inn in Middleburg, Virginia.

DECEMBER

THURSDAY
27

MONDAY
24

FRIDAY
28

TUESDAY
25
CHRISTMAS

SATURDAY
29

WEDNESDAY
26

SUNDAY
30

DECEMBER
JANUARY

MONDAY
31

TUESDAY
1
NEW YEAR'S DAY

WEDNESDAY
2

Children's rocking horses

in a restored log cabin.

<u>THURSDAY</u>
3

<u>F R I D A Y</u>
4

<u>SATURDAY</u>
5

<u>S U N D A Y</u>
6

JANUARY

MONDAY
7

TUESDAY
8

WEDNESDAY
9

A hooked rug, from late-nineteenth-century

Connecticut, in the Tree of Life motif.

THURSDAY
10

FRIDAY
11

SATURDAY
12

SUNDAY
13

With special thanks to:

January 1, April 16, June 25, August 30, November 26
Don Kelly and Warren Fitzsimmons

January 8, October 15, October 22, Notes
Dottie and Mannie Affler

January 15, February 26
Sally Riffle

January 22, July 23, September 24
Beth Gerschall

January 29
Marjorie Staufer

February 5, November 5
Barbara and Fred Johnson

February 12
Barbara Strawser

February 19
Holly Meier

March 12
Diane and Stan Gove

March 19
Beverly Jacomini

March 26, photo at right
Joel and Kate Kopp

March 29, June 11
Carol Pflumm

April 2, August 13
Pat Stauble

April 23
Corrine Burke

Antique wallpaper-covered boxes

and painted wooden birds.

May 7
Pat and Jim Goodman

May 28
Forest Fenn

June 18, August 20, September 17, October 22
Lee Cochran

July 2
Bernard Barenholtz

August 27
Jane and George Harold

October 8
Winendale Historical Center, Round Top, Texas

October 15
Betty Murray

November 12
Helene and Dana Koch

November 19
Barbara Gray

November 22
Barbara and Manus Rogoff

December 3
Betty Murray

December 10
Morgan and Gerri MacWhinnie

December 17
Pat Parker

December 24
Red Fox Inn

December 31
John R. Irwin, Museum of Appalachia

New England salt-glazed pottery in a dry sink cupboard.

NOTES

NOTES

NOTES

NOTES

N O T E S

NOTES

N O T E S

NOTES